IGNORE THE RATTLESNAKE

Ronald N. Goulden, MBA, PMP

Ignore the Rattlesnake
Copyright © 2012
Ronald N. Goulden, MBA, PMP

ALL RIGHTS RESERVED

Cover art by Ronald Goulden

ISBN: 146997987X

Introduction

Over the course of forty years, I have been on both sides of the interview table. As such, I have some unique perspectives on the interview process.

The purpose of this book is to share some of my insights, along with some things to do and to avoid during the job search endeavor.

I will use anecdotes, based on actual interview experiences to illustrate some of my points.

Eventually, you will understand why you '**Ignore the Rattlesnake**'.

In forty years of hiring and being hired, I have NEVER hired a 'loser'…all of my hires have turned into 'superstars' often being hijacked by other managers after seeing the quality of the employees I bring in.

Usually, I have a good feel before bringing anyone in for an interview. Within the first two or three minutes of the interview, I have made my decision.

The key to getting hired is to be memorable (in a favorable way). You want to be the person who comes to mind when the hiring manager starts reviewing resumes or making a job offer. If you are too much like the other three hundred people applying for the same job, you stand a strong chance of being dismissed even before you get an interview.

{While writing this book, my employer of four years decided to 'eliminate' my position. They gave me 25 days notice. By following my own advice from this book, I accepted a job offer, less than two weeks into the job search, with a twenty percent increase in salary.}

Note: This book is intended to provide tips to a job seeker and does not imply any guarantee of employment…that is up to you.

Networking

Probably the single most important thing you can do in your job search is to 'network' with others who may be able to assist in finding a new position. Your network can include friends, recruiters, vendors, and previous employers, supervisors, and co-workers.

In poor economic times, many firms are reluctant to pay recruiting fees and may not even bother to post the jobs on the Internet job boards, opting instead to use a more informal approach to finding quality employees.

By networking with others searching for a job, you can dramatically increase your potential job market. Even though at first glance, it would seem that someone else looking for a job may be a competitor, there is a strong likelihood that they do not work in the same field and will not be in competition with you for a job. That being said, they may come across a job in your field during the course of their job search and may even be able to effect an introduction to the hiring official.

Many communities have scheduled job networking meeting where the participants can share their experiences and leads with others. I find it comforting to talk with other in my situation.

If you are an IT professional and you hear of an accounting position at XYZ company share the lead with those in your network. It may help someone find a job and you will have an ally in XYZ company.

References

Most companies will ask for two or three references during the job process. I do not provide references until the company or interviewer requests them. If they are going to check my references, I take that as a good sign.

Early in the job search phase, contact those you want to use as a reference and ask their permission. *{You do not want to have your reference 'blind-sided' and make an off-the-cuff remark.}* Courtesy demands that you have their permission.

Normally, you will want to have a supervisor, a co-worker, and possibly an outside contact such as a vendor (depending on your job history). The thing about references is that you will not include anyone who might say something detrimental about you...everyone knows this, but the reference check is usually required.

After finding a position, make sure you thank your references for their assistance and willingness to help. (You may need them again, in the near future.)

Drug & Background Checks

Many employers now routinely perform background and drug testing on prospective employees. This booklet will not tell anyone how to live, but a bad result on a drug test can cost the job. The same is true for a background check.

Depending on the company and the position a credit check may be ordered as well. Poor credit and bankruptcies may end the application process.

{At the beginning of the application process, I opt for a policy of full disclosure.} Being upfront saves a lot of time and expense and actually provides an opportunity to 'explain' certain extenuating circumstances (if there are any) and may cause you to 'stand out' in the memory of the interviewer.

Social Media

Social media sites and be a great venue to share experiences and thoughts along with career information. Some sites tend to be more professionally-focused than other sites.

One thing to be aware of is that with increasing frequency, employers are checking candidates' social media entries to obtain more insights into the individual. (It is probably not wise to 'bad mouth' and interviewer on a social site…it might cost you a job.)

{Many attorneys have won court cases by reviewing the social media sites to see what the participants are saying about the case.}

Resumes

In most cases, the resume and cover letter are your first (and only) opportunity to 'open the door' to a new opportunity and employment.

You should have at least two versions of your resume; one which is designed to be attention-grabbing to a living person. Depending upon the profession and your personal inclinations, this may include exotic fonts and formatting, tables, charts, pictures, and graphs.

The second version of your resume should exclude the exotic fonts and formatting, tables, charts, pictures, and graphs. This version will be used for electronic applications and submissions so that scanning software will be able to read your resume.

Before sending your resume, match it with the job description of the position you are applying for. *{Typically, I have a separate resume and cover letter for every position I am interested in.}* While this may seem like a lot of extra work, you ARE trying to obtain a position where you will be doing actual work.

If you are unemployed, your job is to find a job.

By tailoring your resume to meet the requirements of the job description, you are reinforcing your interest in the position and showing the employer how you can meet a defined need.

Photos or Not?

Many people like to include their photo on their resume. *{While this is a matter of personal choice, as an employer, I would rather not know what you look like prior to the interview. I prefer to base my evaluation of you on skills, knowledge, ability, and personality and not be pre-biased in any way by a photo.}*

Depending upon the type of position and the industry, the photo may be perfectly reasonable and expected. In other industries, the photo may get in the way. *{If you are an extremely attractive woman being screened by another woman, your photo may have a negative effect on the selection process. Similarly, if a man selects you based on appearance over abilities, problems may arise.}*

Production Line Resumes

As part of the personalization of your resume to the job description, make sure your resume does not look like it is a 'mass produced' (and mailed) document. *{If I am going to take the time and expend the political equity to consider you for a position in my organization, I want to have 'some' assurance that your are actually applying to my advertised job and not doing a daily email dump on any advertised opening.}*

If your resume looks too 'canned' or too generic, it will be dismissed. If you go to a resume writing service, make sure they tailor your resume to meet your unique qualifications and not merely copy and paste your information into a template that produces the same resume, with only minor changes between your resume and the next. *{I have received resumes so similar that only the names were changed.*

The address and phone numbers were the same, as was ninety-nine percent of the resume body.} This type of resume may work as long as the employer does not receive any of your resume's siblings.

How to Stand Out

One way to make your resume 'stand out' is through proper organization. Typically, a job description will list basic duties, specific duties, and essential requirements. Illustrate your match to the essential requirements, or qualifications immediately below your contact information. This allows the screener to immediately note that you have the skills, education, and background required by the job.

Next, define your skills and experience in terms that directly correlate to the specific duties itemized on the job description (bullet for bullet, if necessary).

Finally, address the basic duties.

Finish your resume with any special activities, skills, or works that may have a bearing on the job.

By following this roadmap, you are answering the questions of the resume screener before they lose interest. *{Normally, my first pass through a resume is less than thirty seconds. If I do not see a good match, that resume goes into my 'dead' pile.}*

Buy Back?

After accepting a position and tendering your resignation, there are instances when your employer will ask you what it will take to keep you. How you respond to this question is an individual choice. Your response, like the offer, can be interpreted two ways.

When an employer makes an offer to 'buy you back'; the offer can be interpreted in two ways.

First, your resignation comes as a surprise to the employer and they honestly want to keep you as an employee.

Second, your resignation comes as a surprise and they do not have a viable replacement for you at that time and want to keep you on board (for a while) until they can train someone to take your place.

When you tender your resignation, you are telling your employer you are unhappy with your employment and seek a 'better' opportunity elsewhere.

In either case, your resignation will be viewed as disloyalty to the company, and depending upon the culture of the company, you may be treated as an 'outcast'.

If you accept an offer to be 'bought back', you are telling the company that you feel their offer will make your working environment better. You are also stating that you have a price.

{The only time I allowed myself to be 'bought back' had less than optimal results. I was offered a $5,000 increase in my annual salary with no change to my duties, responsibilities, or environment. After three months, they replaced me with someone else.

My buy back ruined my relationship with the company that offered me a position and the recruiter who helped my find the position, and grossed me just under $1250 for that time, at the end of which, I found myself looking for a job.}

Raises Are Cheap

An employer can offer any sum of money, but they only have to pay you for what you work. If they offer a $20,000 increase in your annual pay and let you go after three months, it only cost them $5,000 the keep you around until your replacement could be located and trained.

{On the flip side, I 'bought back' a key employee for mutually agreeable terms. While he continued to work (at a reduced level of productivity), he used the time to find an even better opportunity, leaving without any notice.}

Personally, I do not engage in 'buy backs' any more. If I leave…I leave and honor my agreements with recruiter and new employer. If an employee resigns, I wish them the best and start searching for their replacement.

Another 'buy back' negative for the employer is the damage to political equity at the company. If the hiring manager negotiates to accommodate your terms, he or she is gambling that you will honor the agreement. If you still leave after a few weeks or months, the manager who went to bat for you has suffered a potentially career-damaging blow to their reputation within the company.

Recruiters

Recruiters can be valuable assets in the job search… and they can be a hindrance. A good recruiter may have connections and insights into the hiring needs and practices of a specific company or group of companies. They may also have unofficial 'connections' with others in their network who might be searching for help, but cannot afford the fees associated with the normal recruiting process.

On the flip side, a bad recruiter may 'flood' your resume into all of the client companies, essentially creating a conflict that results in your resume being discarded. *{To avoid potential legal and financial complications, most companies will discard resumes and disqualify applicants who are submitted from multiple sources. So if you submit your resume through an Internet Job Board and a recruiter submits your resume as well…you will NOT be considered for the job.}*

When to Use Recruiters

Recruiters ARE valuable resources and should be used when appropriate. If you know that a particular company ONLY hires candidates sponsored by a specific recruiter, then work with that recruiter. However, make sure that the recruiter only submits you to positions and companies with your approval, after discussing the opportunity.

Avoid using a recruiter if you are applying directly to the company or through an Internet Job Site. If you can present yourself, why have someone else do the same thing and charge the company a placement fee?

Recruiter Costs

Recruiters are in business to make money and they do this by providing a 'screening and qualification' service to the hiring company. Most recruiters will interview their candidates and make sure there is a fit between the candidate (you) and the company before setting up an interview.

In tight economic times, the fees associated with recruiters can be burdensome and are avoided by many companies. Typically the fees range from 15% to 40% (but may go higher). These fees add to the initial costs of hiring a person, along with any travel, lodging, meals, etc.).

{That being said, if identical candidates are presented to me, one as a direct application and one represented by a recruiter and both are asking the same salary, the individual represented by the recruiter is at a disadvantage due to the overhead costs of employment. As an

example, at a 20% recruitment fee, a $50k salary is a $10k difference in cost to hire. All other things being equal, I will hire the unrepresented individual. }

If a recruiting firm asks you to pay for their services or to access their 'proprietary' job listings, politely decline and find another firm to work with. Most legitimate recruiting firms derive their income from the companies and not from the unemployed job seekers. (Of course, there may be legitimate exceptions, though in forty years, I have not come across any.)

Contract to Hire?

Some companies are adamant about not paying any recruitment fees. However, in some cases, they ARE willing to pay a slightly higher rate for a Contract to Hire (CTH) relationship. This allows the company to try out the employee for a defined period of time, with an implicit understanding that the contractor will convert to an employee after the contract term.

Typically, at the end of the Contract to Hire term, the employer is free to offer the candidate a permanent position without incurring any addition placement fees.

{Normally, I like to offer a salary/rate equal to or greater than what the candidate was getting through the recruiting firm. This makes a very positive transition for the candidate/employee and demonstrates a degree of fairness.

I have been on contracts where the employer offered me a significant decrease in wages...I had to decline the offer. Three weeks later, I had a position paying twice what was being offered by the first company.}

Internet Job Boards

There are countless jobs boards on the Internet, some are very good and some are not so good. In all my years of seeking jobs, I have never even received a response to the hundreds (thousands?) of resumes I have submitted via an Internet job board.

Some of the better job boards will identify the sponsoring company and I then go directly to the Company web site to apply, bypassing the job board interface whenever possible.

I do post my resume on the job boards, but seldom get any viable job opportunities. Normally, all I get are franchise offers and low-level sales positions (from home).

If you are employed, but searching for a new job; be careful about posting your resume on the job boards. Many employers take offense at their employees searching for a new job and will terminate the employee immediately upon learning of the job search. (This is probably not legal, but they have ways around the laws.)

{When I start a job search while employed (which is typically the first day on the job), I 'sanitize' my resume, making sure anything that identifies me or my current company are not available by using phrases like 'my current company' rather than 'XYZ Company'.}

On-line Applications

Many companies have websites with a 'Careers' link that allows you to search for jobs within their organization. Some of these sites may be very simple and easy to navigate, while others may provide a detailed and comprehensive application process.

Have a 'clean' (no tables, exotic fonts, pictures, charts, etc) version of your resume. Many firms use resume scanning software that reads the content of the resume and matches it with the job description and requirements. Typically, exotic resumes are handled well by this software and may result in your resume being discarded.

One of the Catch-22 items on many on-line applications deals with 'Expected Salary'. If you enter a rate that is too high, there is a probability that your application will be dismissed. If you enter a rate that is too low, you may be short-changing yourself, or lowering your desirability in the eyes of the hiring manager. Perhaps the safest thing to do is to enter your most recent salary.

Differentiators

I've had situations where I've had hundreds of resumes to parse through. I have also been in the situation where I was competing with hundreds of others for the same position. It is always advisable to make your resume 'stand out'; to differentiate yourself from the hundreds of other resumes the interviewer may be reading.

First Resume

Typically, the first resume will be an electronic document emailed or attached as a file.

{As a hiring official, I always insist that Human Resources give me all resumes for my advertised positions...that way, I don't lose a viable candidate over a spelling error or typo (Cobal vs. COBOL). In addition, I may come across a skill set I know I will need for an upcoming position.

When evaluating resumes, I use a highlighter and mark any keywords on the resume that are a direct match for the current position. After scanning the resume, I place it in one of three piles: Keep, Review, Discard.}

The Keep pile is generally the smallest pile and consists of those resumes that are the closest obvious match for my needs.

The Review pile is generally much larger than the Keep pile, but smaller than the Discard pile. It contains resumes that may not be a perfect match, but have some feature that makes me want to give it a second look.

The Discard pile is typically the largest pile, for a number of reasons:

1. *No apparent match with the job requirements*
2. *Under qualified*
3. *Poorly formatted resume*
4. *Lack of seriousness*
5. *The obvious work of a 'resume mill'*

I have seen resumes that looked as if they were produced from the same file...only the contact information changed. If your resume looks just like someone else's, I will probably discard both of them.}

Your job as an applicant is to make your resume standout and grab my attention. Some standards state that the resume should only be one page or should only include the last ten years.

{Frankly, if your resume is well-formatted and coherent, I do not care if it is one or five pages. If you provide enough compelling, RELEVANT information that identifies you as a superior candidate, I will continue to read.}

Make sure you have read the job description and adjusted your resume to coincide with the needs articulated by the job description (or any other reliable information you've gathered).

Having a cogent, attractive resume is only part of the process. If you have published any scholarly articles, include a reference (and link, if it is available on the Internet). If you are sending your resume electronically, consider using hyper-links to make it easy for the hiring official to review tour publications and other online documentation (but do not go overboard).

If you have a vast wealth of experience, garnered over years of working in your field, you may want to summarize these skills in a chart or spreadsheet format to allow the interviewer to quickly assess your experience…include actual 'hands-on' experience in terms of years (or months). Do NOT include operating systems that you've used unless your skills are above average, and they are relevant to the job (more is not always better). Now days, almost everyone has used one or more of the common computer operating systems…listing them on the resume is a waste of space.

Second Resume

The second resume is the one you take to the interview with you. (Always take one or two extras, just in case you get the opportunity to talk with more than a single person.)

Some people like to use 'artistic' paper and backgrounds or include their photo on the resume. *{My opinion is that artistic papers and backgrounds are distracting and it makes me more critical of the resume. Photos are ok, but again, I'm looking to hire your skills, not your appearance; besides, if I am interviewing you, I will know what you look like, so the picture may just be a waste of space.}*

Use a good weight white or cream paper for your resume. If you want to make it stand out, include a professional pocket folder with your presentation quality resume on one side with any attachments on the other side. These attachments are your 'leave behinds'.

{From my experience, if you give me a clean resume in a nice presentation folder…I WILL review it after the interview, unless you have just totally 'blown' the interview.}

The more times your resume or name crosses the hiring official's desk, the better your chances are. A variety of 'Leave Behinds' can produce surprising results.

{Prior to one interview, I had worked up a sample Work Breakdown Structure (WBS) spreadsheet document for a Project Management class…I included a copy in my resume packet that I delivered to the CIO and the hiring director. The CIO was so taken with the WBS that he offered the job on the spot, because it was a document his bosses could understand.}

A business card is a simple reminder that fits nicely in a pocket or sits comfortably on the top of a keyboard. You can print your own, order some on the Internet, or go to a Brick & Mortar printer and have them produced for less than a hundred dollars. I always include one in my resume packet. *{I use both side of the card: the front side contains contact information and the back side is a bulleted list of skills and achievements.}*

If you have published any works related to your industry or to the job position, include a sample. May hiring officials have a desire to become published, but may lack the time to follow that desire. If you are a published author, you may strike a familiar chord with the interviewer.

If possible, provide a summary of your relevant skills as a document separate from your resume. With proper formatting, the interviewer can quickly assess your capabilities as they may relate to upcoming job requirements.

{I developed a program that I use to track the skills of my employees and can print a nicely formatted skills summary, indicating the skill by number of years experience with that skill. This can be replicated using a spreadsheet.}

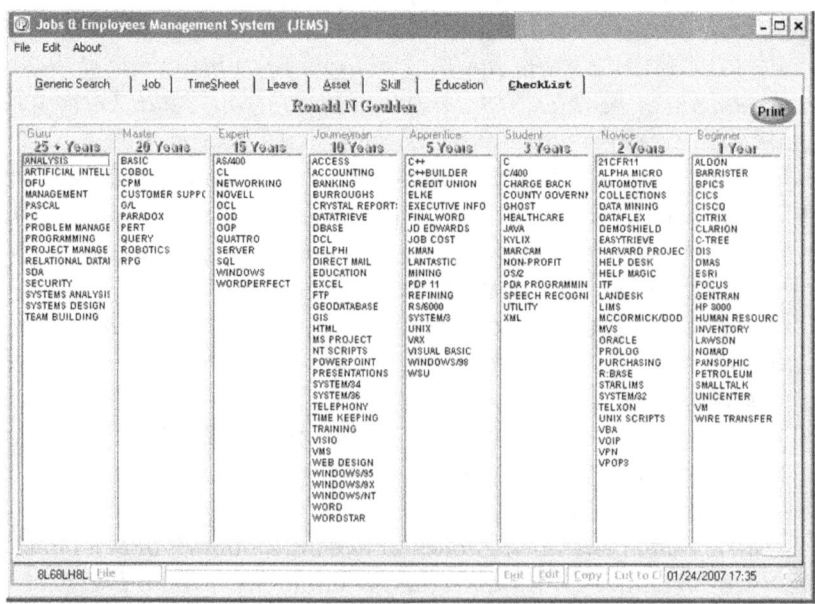

You want to leave a positive lasting image. If you are asked about your most challenging/enjoyable/memorable/etc job experience, provide an anecdote that goes beyond the "I managed a project that saved $100 k per year…"

{On one of my jobs, I was the IT Director for a large mining company. As part of the plant automation process, I had to install telemetry on key components of the refinery…one of which was the hoist. Due to the nature of my staff, I was the only able-bodied person capable and the plant electricians refused to help because it was 'computer stuff'. So I climbed to the top of the fifty foot hoist, which cycled sixteen tons every forty-five seconds. I would work furiously, tightening the bolts while counting 42…43…44… hugging the frame of the hoist for dear life every forty-five seconds as it shook vigorously, threatening to hurl me to the ground four stories below. The interviewer listed with wide-eyed, rapt attention…I knew he would remember me.}

Which story would you remember; the $100k savings or the image of being shaken from a trembling hoist as you tried to do your job? If you follow this course, make sure the story is true and that you can relate to some desirable business trait.

The Interview

There are two schools of thought about interviews. The most common view is to only interview for jobs you are actually (marginally) qualified for and have a desire to win. The newer school of thought is to interview as much as possible. *{Personally, I take offense with this viewpoint. When I decide to bring someone for an interview, it is because I have a legitimate interest in hiring that person. Depending on the situation, I may expend considerable financial and political capital to bring someone in, especially if the candidate is from out of town. (There are obvious recruiting costs such as: travel, lodging, food and hiring costs like as relocation expenses.) So, if I am serious enough to ask you to interview for a position with my company, I would expect you to be equally serious and not simply view me as 'interview experience' or a free trip.}*

If you are not interested in actually accepting a legitimate offer for employment, do not ask me to waste my time and equity considering you for the position.

If your resume is polished enough and stands out enough, you may be granted an interview. The first interview may merely be a phone interview to screen candidates for the second round of face-to-face interviews.

If you are at home, make sure you are in a quiet, 'professional' environment (no lawn mowers, screaming kids, loud music, etc). You are trying to convince someone to hire you... have the courtesy to display a little professionalism. Nothing can destroy a phone interview like distracting background noise.

{I interviewed one young lady for an EDI position. Her resume was superb and the phone interview went extremely well. I invited her in for a face-to-face interview. She came into the room shook hands; then slouched so low in the chair that I thought she was going to slide out of the chair and onto the floor. Her responses were slow and lethargic and lacked the vibrancy she exhibited on the phone. Finally, I asked her if she was interested in the job. Her response was, "Why? Are you offering it to me?" She did not get the job. To this day, I wonder if someone else handled the phone interview for her.}

Interview for the job you are interviewing for

When you actually have the opportunity to interview...take time to review the job description and any relevant notes or research. While confidence is a good thing in an interview, arrogance can be devastating. You have to walk a thin line between confidence and arrogance.

If you are interviewing for a Help Desk technician position, do not try to 'talk' you way into a manager's role.

{I was interviewing a series of people for a Help Desk technician position. As part of a training process, I had my Help Desk manager participate in the interview. During the course of the interview, the candidate 'took charge' of the interview and laid out complex plans about how he was going to restructure the Help Desk and impose Service Level Agreements on our users and define performance metrics for the staff. Since I had already made my decision about the gentleman, I allowed him to proceed for a few minutes before cutting him off. In response to another question, he again began asserting how he would change the entire Help Desk operation.

After the interview, the Help Desk manager and I reviewed notes. He said that he really liked the candidate and wanted to make an offer. I responded that I would be happy to, but I would have to let him (the Help Desk manager) go, since the candidate was interviewing for his job and not the advertised Help Desk technician position.}

Go into every interview confident (without ANY arrogance) that you will walk away with the job...the confidence will show through in the interview. Every Job I landed over forty years was because I 'knew' going into the interview that I was the best candidate.

Do not presume to know enough to change my business during the interview

Again, confidence is a wonderful trait to bring to an interview…but avoid arrogance and pre-conceived ideas. While you may have great ideas and bring a wealth of experience, remember that you are interviewing for a position with an existing company that has established processes, procedures, and culture. Do not assume that you, as a job candidate and outsider, can mandate how to change a company. (Besides, if you have truly great ideas to improve the company, do not give it away; use your ideas as negotiating tools.)

{When I was interviewing a Programmer Analyst for a Delphi shop, I went through my introductory overview of the company and its industry-leading technology provided by the Delphi programming language and how we have used it to keep at the forefront of our industry for fifteen years.

The candidate spent the next thirty minutes explaining how he was a Basic programmer and had worked for years converting other applications to Basic. When I re-iterated that we were a Delphi programming shop, he calmly advised me that we would have to change and that he would convert our legacy system to Basic in six months.

When I commented that he had no industry-specific experience with our business, he replied that industry experience was unnecessary.}

In the computer industry, it takes months for an individual to learn the specifics of a new company or industry, company culture, and processes and procedures. *{Anytime an individual comes into an interview with a preconceived concept of how to improve the business, I become very wary.}*

Confidence and self-assurance are great, but over-confidence is obnoxious.

Phones

Unless you are expecting a medical emergency, turn your phone off or leave it in the car. If you do expect a legitimate medical emergency, advise the interviewer at the outset of the interview.

{I interviewed one gentleman who wore his Bluetooth headset during the entire process (I'm a patient and understanding individual who often 'accommodates' the idiosyncrasies of others). He lost the interview when he held his hand up for me to stop talking as he responded to the conversation on the Bluetooth. He did not get the job.}

If someone feels their phone is too important to put aside for an hour, what kind of worker are they going to be? I do not want to hire someone who will be on their cell phone or have a blue tooth stuck in their ear all day.

{In fact, If someone walks into a meeting wearing a blue-tooth, I dismiss them from the meeting. Constant attention to personal cell phones is not appropriate.}

Attire

Dress for the position you are interviewing for, or better. While you may sometimes overdress for a position, it is not as interview-ending as under-dressing. *{Being kind of 'old-school' I typically wear a suit, tie, and cufflinks to my interviews. If the interviewer comments about being over-dressed, I simply respond that I am 'old school' and would rather not be disrespectful by assuming a lesser dress code for the interview.}*

However, if you are interviewing for a blue collar position, a suit might be completely inappropriate. Sometimes, it is legitimate to ask about the interview dress code, and plan on dressing above the level indicated.

{I interviewed one for a programming position which clearly stated on the job description that the dress code was 'business casual'. He walked in wearing a dirty tee-shirt, cut-offs, and flip-flops. Guess who did not get the job.}

Posture

During the interview, your posture can say a lot about your interest in the position. If you are slouched in your chair or slumped over the table, you may display a lack of interest.

{While I do not expect candidates to lean forwards and 'hang breathlessly' on my every word, I do expect them to display a basic level of attention and interest.}

If the candidate slouches back in the chair, puts his ankle on his knee, rocks the chair back and forth, it sends a message to the interviewer that there is no legitimate level of interest in the job or the interview.

Attitude

Your attitude and win or lose the job for you. You do need to remember that you are trying to get a position with the company and as such, you are at somewhat of a disadvantage.

Do not try to take over the interview, but do not wait passively for the next question. Ideally, an interview should be a two-way 'conversation between you and the hiring official.

{When I have a candidate try to dominate my interview, forcing me to follow their 'script', I become suspicious that they are not qualified for the job and hope to 'baffle me' until the time allotted for the interview expires.}

Do not 'argue' with the interviewer…it will be self-defeating, even if you win the argument. Some people are unable to allow errors and lapses to slip and must confront the person directly to correct their error. Do not do this. If an interviewer makes an obvious mistake, ignore it and move on, unless he is misstating information you have provided.

"Tell me about yourself"

This is a common interview question and I often use it to buy time to perform a quick review of the resume. Current wisdom advises you to use a 'sixty-second commercial' to highlight your match with the job description or to provide a quick summary of reasons for me to hire you.

{I look at it differently. I use this as an opportunity to give the interviewer something he or she has never heard before. I provide an anecdote that illustrates my value or attitude without actually phrasing it in terms of business processes. I call it my 'Rattlesnake speech'.

On the job in Carlsbad, New Mexico, where I was the IT Director, I had to install telemetry on key components in the refinery. Since I was the only able-bodied IT person capable and the plant electricians refused to help because it was 'computer stuff', I took it upon myself to grab my tools and crawl under the grating of the raised floor of the outdoor refinery.

I was on my back, working diligently, adjusting and tightening the device to a motor frame when I heard a loud 'buzzing' coming from the direction of my right foot. I paused long enough to look around, thinking there might be an electrical 'arc' I would need to report to the maintenance crews. Instead, I saw an angry, five foot long diamondback rattlesnake informing me of his displeasure.}

The hiring official stopped man and asked, "What did you do?"

*{My response was that I had a job to finish, so I chose to "**Ignore the Rattlesnake**". By the time I finished my work, the reptile calmed down and moved to another area under the refinery flooring.*

While this anecdote did not have any 'real' relevance to the job, it illustrated that I was the type of person who would take all necessary steps to finish an assigned task.

I had the job offer the day after the interview.}

The 'moral' of the anecdote is that I set myself apart from ANY other candidate, in a way none of them could match. When it came time for the hiring official to evaluate candidates, I wanted an unforgettable 'hook', *(Who could forget the 'rattlesnake guy'?)*

Everyone has a unique story from their past that can be spun into a relevant job asset or characteristic, think about something to tell if the opportunity arises. While it may not always work, it works for me. *{Having a pocket full of 'adventures' makes it easy for me to provide an anecdote and figure a way to relate it to a job.}* Just make sure your anecdote is true.

"What would it take to succeed in this job?"

Recruiters and employment counselors always tell you to 'ask for the job". Show an interest in the job. You should always have two or three prepared questions to ask in the interview process. Most interviewers will prompt you to ask any questions you might have. It is advisable to ask SOMETHING. *{I typically ask about any pending legislation or litigation that might affect the future plans or stability of the company.}*

But one of the most important questions to ask is along the lines of **"What will it take to succeed in this job?"** (Or **"What are the three critical success factors for this position?"** These questions give the interviewer the opportunity to expound on any mistakes the predecessor may have made, or what he hopes this position to evolve into.

Post Interview

The more times your names comes across the desk of the hiring official, the better off you are…to a point. While you want your name to surface to the top of the pile, try not to be too obnoxious or overbearing.

There will come a point of diminishing returns with your communications and when you sense that the interviewer may be approaching impatience, reduce the communications…it may be a lost cause. <u>You will not get every job you interview for</u>.

Thank you letter/email

It is always advisable to send a thank you letter as soon after the interview as possible…unless you do not want the job. Then, it's just a matter of courtesy…after all; the interviewer did take time to consider you for the job.

Besides, the 'Thank you' letter gets your name in front of the interviewer and provides an opportunity (without pressure) to explain an interview response that needs more clarification (or to recover from a nervous mistake).

After a week

If you have not heard back from the interviewer after a week, there is a distinct possibility that you are not being considered for the position. However, it may be that the interviewer is extremely busy and has not had time to finalize the decision/offer.

One way to probe for the status is to send a follow-up letter asking about the status of your interview, re-iterating your interest in the position and adding 'after-thought' responses or clarifications. It is always good to offer to provide any additional information desired.

Do not get carried away by burying the interviewer with emails and letters and phone calls. While you need to get a job, the interviewer has a job beyond merely hiring someone. If you are too aggressive, you may talk yourself out of a job.

The Job Offer

When a job is offered, especially after an extended search, the first inclination is to immediately accept and run out the door to celebrate. Please do not do so.

Unless it is a 'take-it-or-leave-it' job offer that you have to accept on the spot, ask for a day or two to discuss it with your family. Most employers are amenable to this and often make an offer on a Friday so the candidate has the week-end to think about it. *{Be aware that employers WANT you to be sure about your decision. Recruiting and interviewing is expensive and employers want to hire someone who will stay and be productive for them.}*

Compensation

Unless the salary and benefits have been discussed early in the interview or job posting process, the matter of compensation will arise. Current wisdom states that the first one to name a figure is at the disadvantage. It is always best to get the interviewer to make the first salary offer; that way, you can then determine if it is in the range you were expecting or engage in some additional negotiation *{just make sure you do not 'negotiate' yourself out of the job}*.

Typically, the opening will come in the form of a question, "What will it take to get you to work for us?" Be aware that the amount you specify will probably be the high mark for the salary negotiation and may likely be scaled down from there. *{Try to respond in a non-committal manner along the lines of, "I bring a lot to the table, and I would expect to receive a fair market salary for my contributions."}*

If the salary if firmly fixed with no room for adjustment, try to negotiate for additional benefits such as an extra week of vacation, tuition reimbursement, stocks, etc. You may not get them, but at least you've tried. *{In several instances, the hiring officials were locked into a starting salary. I suggested a salary starting at that point with a guaranteed performance and salary review after ninety days. That gave the hiring officials the opportunity to benefit from my performance and contributions for three months. In every case, I was granted a raise equal to what I requested in the initial salary negotiations. }*

The New Job

After landing a new job, almost everyone makes the same mistake; they neglect the most important first task.

The first thing anyone should do after starting a new job is to update their resume immediately to reflect the new company and responsibilities, while the job description is still uppermost in the mind. *{If you doubt the importance of keeping your resume up-to-date, just think back on your recent experience with unemployment, Typically, writing and updating the resume is one of the most difficult tasks in the job search.}*

Keep your resume current; in the current environment, there may be no warning when a company is bought, sold, shut down, or forced to lay-off. By having your resume current, you have a jump on other job seekers.

Remember that there is no real loyalty to employees anymore and the perfect job you expect to retire from may vanish tomorrow. Always be searching for that better job.

###

Other books
by
Ronald Goulden

Learn Excel
with the Quality Scorecard

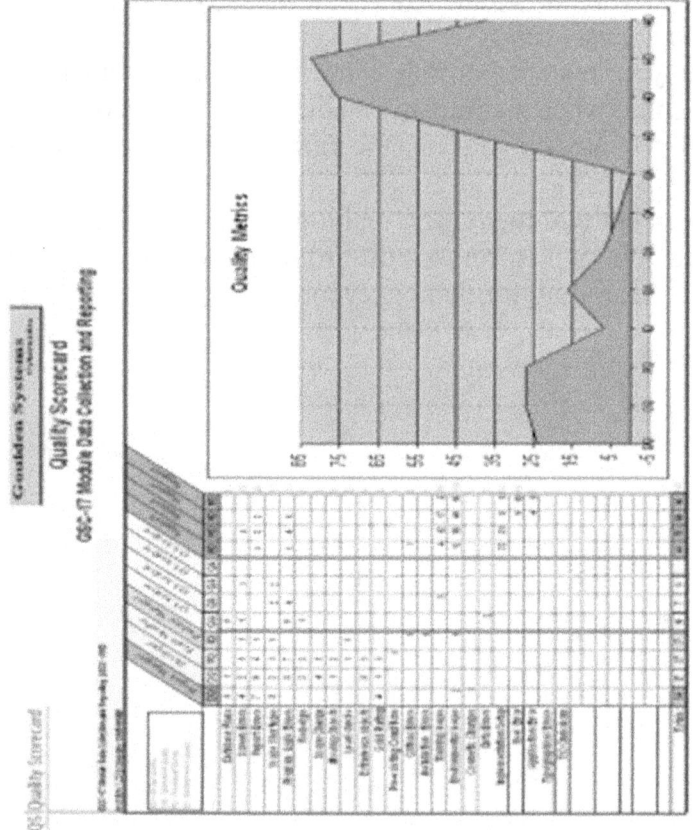

A Build-a-Tool Module

Ronald N. Goulden, MBA, PMP

There are a lot of books about learning Microsoft® Excel. This is yet another such book though one with a bit of a twist. The process of this book will start with a blank worksheet and develop it into a sophisticated Project Management tool called the 'Quality Scorecard'.

Do not be alarmed if you are not a Project Manager, the Scorecard can be used in other realms, limited only by your imagination. At the very least, this exercise will illustrate the capabilities of Excel and teach some valuable techniques in the process.

The book assumes the reader knows nothing about Excel and progressively elaborates upon each exercise and technique, building knowledge while providing insights into how to make Excel work for you. It will not overpower you with advanced techniques and vague tips that you may never use.

Each subsequent chapter will build on previous work so that by the end of the book, you will have a fully functional (and modifiable) Quality Scorecard and an understanding of how it works.

The concepts learned here will be valuable in any context. There is no requirement for VBA or Macro programming for these exercises.

The final chapter will be a discussion of the Concept of 'Quality by Design', which is the foundation of the Quality Scorecard.

Learn Excel:
Executive Summary & Scope

A Build-a-Tool Module

Ronald N. Goulden, MBA, PMP

http://www.amazon.com/dp/1467905356/

This is the second book in the "Build-A-Tool' series of books for learning Microsoft® Excel while creating fully functional Project Management tools (which, with a little ingenuity, can be applied to other fields of study). The process of this book will start with blank worksheets and develop them into sophisticated Project Management tools called the 'Executive Summary" and Scope" documents. There are three bonus tools included in this module: "The Cover Sheet", the

"Charter', and the "Cost Baseline". Together, these five documents provide the foundation for the Prospectus package to be presented to executive management for project approval.

Do not be alarmed if you are not a Project Manager, these tools can be used in other realms, limited only by your imagination. At the very least, this exercise will illustrate the capabilities of Excel and teach some valuable techniques in the process. There is no need to learn Visual Basic for Applications (VBA) or macro programming; everything is accomplished with readily available Excel functions.

The book assumes the reader knows little or nothing about Excel and progressively elaborates upon each exercise and technique, building knowledge while providing insights into how to make Excel work for you. It will not overpower you with advanced techniques and vague tips that you may never use.

Each subsequent chapter will build on previous work so that by the end of the book, you will have a fully functional (and modifiable) Cover Sheet, Executive Summary, Scope, Charter, and Cost Baseline and an understanding of how they work.

The concepts learned here will be valuable in any context.

The final chapter will be a discussion of how to combine other "Build-A-Tool" modules into a 'master' template

Project Management
for a Functional World

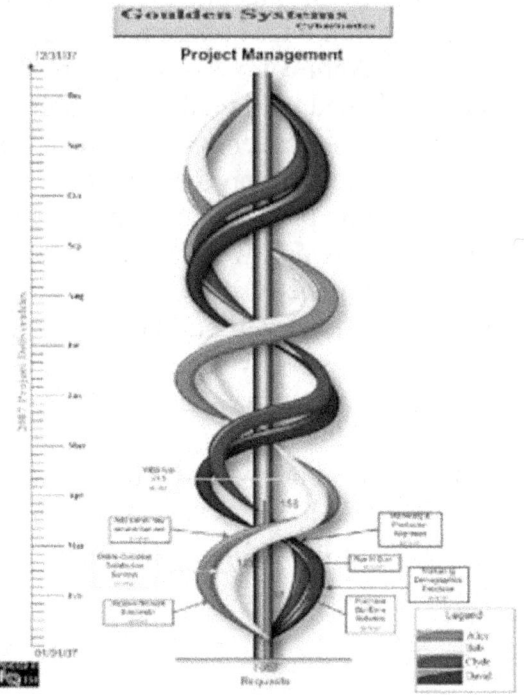

Ronald N. Goulden, MBA, PMP

http://www.amazon.com/dp/1449996590/

The intent of this book is not to be a rehashed version of The Project Management Institute's (PMI®) Project Management Body of Knowledge (PMBOK®). Many excellent books already address these topics very well. The intent of this book is to provide some assistance and insights for Project Managers who might find themselves overwhelmed by the PMBOK®, or a new Project Manager who wants some help getting started and getting organized.

The goal of this book is to provide some insights and guidance for those Project Managers who find themselves managing projects in a functional or weak matrix organizational structure; organizational structures in which the Project Manager has little if any official authority or power. Typically, these will be organizations that have gained a nebulous realization of the benefits of Project Management; but have not committed to converting to a strong matrix or project-based organizational structure.

This book takes the readers beyond the theoretical aspects of Project Management and introduces them to some practical applications of the trade. While much of the focus of this book will be on the Information Technology industry; the tips, tools, and techniques introduced here can apply to any project in any industry and will support revenue projects as well as development projects.

www.ingramcontent.com/pod-product-compliance
Lightning Source LLC
Chambersburg PA
CBHW071602170526
45166CB00004B/1759

* 9 7 8 1 4 6 9 9 7 9 8 7 8 *